Creating the Constitution

Other titles in *The Constitution:*

The First Amendment
Freedom of Speech, Religion, and the Press
ISBN: 0-89490-897-9

The Second Amendment
The Right to Own Guns
ISBN:0-89490-925-8

The Fourth Amendment
Search and Seizure
ISBN: 0-89490-924-X

The Fifth Amendment
The Right to Remain Silent
ISBN: 0-89490-894-4

The Thirteenth Amendment
Ending Slavery
ISBN: 0-89490-923-1

The Fifteenth Amendment
African-American Men's Right to Vote
ISBN: 0-7660-1033-3

The Eighteenth and Twenty-First Amendments
Alcohol—Prohibition and Repeal
ISBN: 0-89490-926-6

The Nineteenth Amendment
Women's Right to Vote
ISBN: 0-89490-922-3

Creating the Constitution

The People and Events That Formed the Nation

The Constitution

Daniel Weidner, Ed. D.

Enslow Publishers, Inc.

40 Industrial Road   PO Box 38
Box 398   Aldershot
Berkeley Heights, NJ 07922   Hants GU12 6BP
USA   UK

http://www.enslow.com

Dedicated to: Elisabeth, for so much enthusiasm, Megan Winter for the idea, and those who would learn from it.

Library of Congress Cataloging-in-Publication Data

Weidner, Daniel W.
    Creating the Constitution : the people and events that formed the nation / Daniel Weidner.
        p. cm. — (The Constitution)
        Summary: Explores the creation of the United States Constitution, including the people involved, the ratification process, and the implications for the nation's government, both at its inception and today.
        Includes bibliographical references and index.
        ISBN 0-7660-1905-5
        1. United States—Politics and government—1775-1783—Juvenile literature. 2. United States—Politics and government—1783-1789—Juvenile literature. 3. United States. Constitutional Convention (1787)—Juvenile literature.
4. United States. Constitution—Juvenile literature.
5. Constitutional history—United States—Juvenile literature.
[1. United States—Politics and govenent—1775-1783.
2. United States—Politics and government—1783-1789.
3. United States. Constitutional Convention (1787) 4. United States. Constitution. 5. Constitutional history.]
        I. Title. II. Series.
        E303.W44 2002
        342.73'029—dc21   2002007960

Printed in the United States of America

10 9 8 7 6 5 4 3 2

To Our Readers: We have done our best to make sure all Internet addresses in this book were active and appropriate when we went to press. However, the author and the publisher have no control over and assume no liability for the material available on those Internet sites or on other Web sites they may link to. Any comments or suggestions can be sent by e-mail to comments@enslow.com or to the address on the back cover.

Illustration Credits: Enslow Publishers, Inc., p. 10; John Grafton, *Pictorial Sourcebook of Copyright Free Graphics,* 1974 Dover Publications, NY, pp. 18, 32; Library of Congress, pp. 8, 15, 67, 70, 74, 78; National Archives, pp. 39, 41; Reproduced from the *Dictionary of American Portraits,* Published by Dover Publications, Inc., in 1967, pp. 24, 26, 31, 46, 59, 60, 63.

Cover Illustration: National Archives

Contents

The Articles of Confederation

1

In 1774, a group of American men gathered to talk about a growing indignity—the intolerable acts of the King of England, George III. The group met on September 5 and spent six weeks planning their response to the increasing demands from England, their mother country. Their outrage with England had been building throughout the past ten years. Before that, as a British colony, the American colonies had generally enjoyed the right to pursue their lives with little interference from Great Britain.

In 1763, George III tightened political control over the thirteen colonies of Massachusetts, New Hampshire, Rhode Island, New York, Connecticut, New Jersey, Pennsylvania, Delaware, Maryland, Virginia, North Carolina, South Carolina, and Georgia. He demanded that they pay taxes for their defense and return revenue (percentage of profits) to the mother country. Since the colonies had no voice in British Parliament, this was taxation without representation and it outraged the thirteen colonies. At the time the

The American colonists complained to King George III about
their treatment by his administration.

colonies had no centralized government or doctrine. Each colony acted independently of the other and all, to this point, answered only to the King of England. Their anger with England, however, united them.

Each of the American colonies except Georgia sent delegates to the 1774 meeting and much was accomplished there. The delegates created an Association to oppose the British and to boycott British imports. They also adopted resolutions, called the Declaration of Rights and Grievances, listing and defining the rights of the people and colonies. They agreed to call another Congress if the King did not respond to their grievances to their satisfaction.

British Parliament swiftly rejected the American document. When the Second Continental Congress convened on May 10, 1775, the group was angry and seeking action. They raised military forces and appointed a Commander in Chief—Virginian George Washington—in charge. The Congress established trade regulations and authorized the issuance of money. It established ambassadors to travel to other nations for support, and urged the colonies to set up organized local governments. The Second Congress signed the Declaration of Independence in July, 1776, and adjourned on December 12, 1776. Members of the Congress soon came to believe it should legalize the new powers it had established by providing an official document. The Second Congress organized a committee and appointed John Dickinson as committee head, on July 12, 1776, to draft the Articles of Confederation.

The Third Continental Congress convened just eight days later, on December 20, 1776. This Congress prosecuted the war and made the final adjustments to the Articles of Confederation. On November 15, 1777, the Articles were proposed to the colonies. The

Articles originally proposed by Dickinson and his committee went through many changes before being passed on to the colonies. The Articles originally called for a strong central government, a feature that was later eliminated. In addition, the Articles formally changed the designation of the colonies to States.

Because of the war, and disagreements between the colonies, it took three and a half years to get final ratification of the Articles, which had to be ratified by each and every state. Seven states held claims to western lands. As long as they did, the six states without

Under the Articles of Confederation, the thirteen original states were united in a loose union.

such claims refused to ratify the Articles. To solve this problem, the seven with claims gave up their lands to the newly formed nation, or Union.

Final ratification came on March 1, 1781. The next day, Congress assembled under the new form of government. (The War ended two years later, in April, 1783.)

The Articles created a Confederation called the United States of America. In a confederation, the individual political units (the States), maintain their sovereignty. Each state essentially is its own nation. The states then join together only to deal with certain issues, such as security.

Under the Articles of Confederation, legislatures of the states gave their word that the citizens of every state would be treated without discrimination, that they would give full faith and credit to recognize national legal acts and proceedings, and that they would extradite (return) fugitives wanted in another state. Aside from these matters, the Articles of Confederation provided little structure for the national government.

The Articles of Confederation Government

All governments perform three functions: legislative (law making), executive (running the government and enforcing the laws), and judicial (interpreting the law). In the United States, the legislative functions were given to a Congress made up of one house. There were two to seven representatives from each state who were elected by their state legislatures. States could not send fewer than two or more than seven. No delegate could serve more than three years out of six or serve as an officer under the United States at the same time as being a delegate. The delegates to the Congress were paid by their own states and the states could recall their representatives at any time. The fewer delegates sent, the less the cost to a state. As a result, at certain times, some states had no representatives at all. To make matters worse, since each state had one vote, regardless of its number of representatives, ill feeling soon grew between the large (more populous) and the small (less populous) states. The large states felt that the small states had too much power.

Executive functions were also left in the hands of Congress, rather than with a president or other individual. This would turn out to be a severe weakness of the Articles of Confederation. Unlike a president, a large body needs to debate and vote on issues before it can operate even simple functions. Lengthy debate prevents quick decision making and independent action.

Judicial functions were left to the states rather than the national government. However, Congress did have the power to act as a court to settle disputes that arose between different states.

Weaknesses of the Articles

Throughout the eight years that the Articles of Confederation were in place, numerous weaknesses became obvious. First, the United States was a confederation (alliance). Separate political units (the states) were united for common purposes, but they did not give up their major powers to the central government. The states remained independent and they did not owe total loyalty to the central government. They could withdraw from the political union at any time, if they chose.

Second, Congress did not have the power to collect taxes. It could merely send requests to the state legislatures and hope they would respond. Voluntary contributions by the states were the only source of national income. This proved to be a real problem. The states, which were suffering terrible financial conditions after the Revolutionary War, rarely chose to give up their own money to help the national government.

Congress could not enforce obedience to the laws it passed. It could ask each state for its quota of soldiers, for example, but if the state refused to honor such requests, there was nothing Congress could do.

Each state regulated its own customs duties (taxes), not only on goods imported from foreign countries, but also on imports from other states. Most people were loyal only to their home state. Other states were, for all intents and purposes, like foreign countries. It seemed impossible to create a sense of national pride in the people.

The Articles of Confederation Congress had treaty-making power. It could not make any agreement that restricted the power of the individual states to control both foreign and domestic commerce. Because of this, foreign nations were hesitant to negotiate trade treaties with the United States. They knew such agreements could not be enforced.

Powers granted to the central government had been given to "Congress assembled." That is, the government was a single body. There was no separation or division of authority among different branches. The Continental Congress exercised all national power, yet the power to enforce the laws it made remained in the hands of the individual states.

The method of voting also hindered Congress and limited its ability to act. Each of the thirteen states, regardless of size, had one vote. In order to pass any law, nine votes were needed. To change the Articles of

Confederation, the unanimous consent of the state legislatures was necessary. After the Treaty of Paris, which ended the American Revolution in 1783, a unanimous vote by the Congress was required to change the Articles. This proved impossible in passing even simple laws.

Problems Among the States

After the American Revolution, many difficulties arose between and among the new United States. There were frequent struggles over western lands. Some states claimed the same territory, and disputes arose over the use of rivers for transportation. Sound money (good, valuable money supported by gold or silver) had almost disappeared from circulation. In some places, the people who owed money were in open revolt. During and after the Revolution, the states created their own money, which often decreased in value. Many people, especially farmers, owed money and found it difficult or impossible to repay. Their frustration led to revolt. One was Shays' Rebellion, an uprising of Massachusetts farmers that took place in 1786 and 1787. Angry farmers rose up to try to stop tax collectors and courts from seizing their property as payment for debt.

States also passed laws against one another. Goods moving between states were taxed as though each was a foreign country. If the United States hoped to be united truly as one nation, then it was important for representatives from each of the states to end or reduce tensions between them.

Early Conferences

For years, there had been trouble between Maryland and Virginia over their boundary and commercial

Members of the Regulator movement sometimes turned to violence to express their feelings about the money situation in Massachusetts. Here, a member of the movement attacks a tax collector.

relations. In 1785, a conference was held at Alexandria, Virginia, between delegates representing the two states. This conference adjourned to Mount Vernon (the home of George Washington). There, Virginia's delegates proposed holding yet another conference, to which all the states would be invited. This meeting would consider matters relating to the trade and commerce of all thirteen states.

This second conference was held at Annapolis, Maryland, on September 14, 1786. The delegates of only five states attended. Those who were present passed a resolution to hold a third conference to consider changing and improving the Articles of Confederation.

On February 21, 1787, Congress discussed a proposal calling for a national convention to meet in Philadelphia, Pennsylvania, to work on changes to the Articles of Confederation. After some delay and a good deal of debate, both in Congress and in the state legislatures, the resolution passed. Congress did, however, carefully stipulate that the delegates were to meet, for:

> the sole purpose of revising the Articles of Confederation, and reporting to Congress and the several Legislatures, such alterations and provisions therein, as shall, when agreed to in Congress, and confirmed by the States, render the Federal Constitution adequate to the exigencies of Government, and the preservation of the Union.[1]

Several state legislatures followed Virginia's lead and selected distinguished men to be their delegates to the Philadelphia Convention even before Congress had actually authorized the meeting. Eventually, twelve of the thirteen states decided to send delegates to this third conference. Rhode Island was the only state not represented. The convention would be held in Philadelphia, starting on May 14, 1787.

The Meeting That Changed the Nation

2

Lack of interest throughout the states prevented the Philadelphia Convention from meeting on time. By the opening date there were too few present to hold a meeting. Of the seventy-four delegates selected to go to the convention, only fifty-five ever attended. Thirty-nine of these took leading roles. The average number of delegates at meetings was about thirty. Those who considered it important enough to attend became the "Founding Fathers" of the United States of America.

Members of the Convention

Those who met in Philadelphia were a select group of experienced and educated men. There were seven former governors, thirty-nine men who had served in Congress, and eight other delegates who had experience in writing constitutions for their states. The youngest delegate was twenty-six years old, six were under thirty-one, and only twelve were over the age of fifty-four.

The oldest member of the convention was Pennsylvania's Benjamin Franklin. At eighty-one, Franklin was already famous as a printer, inventor,

Pennsylvania's Benjamin Franklin was the oldest member of the Constitutional Convention.

and for his work in government. His humorous and keen remarks often broke tension and overcame bitterness between opposing delegates.

Franklin's fellow delegate from Pennsylvania, Scottish-born lawyer James Wilson, read most of Franklin's speeches to the convention. He had signed the Declaration of Independence and was a representative to the Continental Congress from Pennsylvania. His inconspicuous work on the Convention's Committee on Detail is considered very important.

Thirty-five-year-old Gouverneur Morris, Pennsylvania's third delegate, was a sharp contrast to witty and wise Benjamin Franklin. Unlike Franklin, who was a champion of the common man, Morris had strong upper-class sympathies. An interesting and eloquent speaker, Morris addressed the convention more often than any other delegate.

Delegate James Madison from Virginia was the best prepared. At five foot four inches tall, he was not an imposing figure, but what he lacked in physical stature he made up in intellect. He had studied the governments of the world, and he brought to the convention a plan for changing the United States greatly. The convention met nearly every weekday for sixteen weeks. Throughout that time, James Madison kept a record of the convention's work. His notes would someday be invaluable to historians studying the work of the convention.

George Washington, whose fame and prestige were already legendary, was unanimously selected as the presiding officer of the convention. His name and character lent great dignity to the proceedings. Although he was very reluctant to attend the Convention, he gave in when others stressed that his presence was needed for it to be successful.

Although its members were noteworthy, missing from the Convention were a number of equally well-known men from the American Revolution. Among these were the fiery Patrick Henry, pamphleteer Thomas Paine, Massachusetts patriots Samuel and John Adams and John Hancock, and Declaration of Independence author Thomas Jefferson. Patrick Henry, though selected, refused to attend. He was opposed to revising the Articles of Confederation. He reportedly stated that he "smelt a rat" in the plan to make changes to the government.[1] Jefferson and John Adams could not attend because they were abroad, working as representatives of the United States in Europe. Thomas Paine had gone to England, and neither John Hancock nor Samuel Adams had been chosen as delegates by their states.

The Convention Begins

While the early arriving delegates waited in Philadelphia, those from Virginia saw their opportunity. They would propose a plan that would help build a strong central government. Those who did not favor a strong national government would later find they were unable to stem the tide.

The convention met for the first time on Friday, May 25, 1787, behind closed doors. There was a reason for the security measures they took to keep the public away. The members did not want the general population to know what they were doing and perhaps create chaos.

The delegates to the convention in Philadelphia carried with them instructions to make some changes in the system of the American government. In defiance of those directions, together, these men would create an entirely new government, which would go on to become a model for struggling democracies around the world.

The Framing of the Constitution

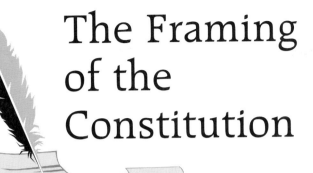

The Continental Congress instructed members of the convention simply to consider amending the Articles of Confederation. The convention was not supposed to make radical changes in the existing system of government. The Framers had a variety of their own opinions about the future of the Articles.

Interests and Agreements

Most delegates to the Philadelphia Convention were professionals: lawyers, merchants, Southern planters, and other large property owners. Collectively, these men made up the colonial aristocracy (upper-class property owners). Almost all owned western lands, government bonds, or private mortgages. These men stood to gain from a powerful national government that would be able to make trade agreements with foreign nations for better prices. In fact, the policies set by the new government that eventually arose from the Constitution helped many of these men make or expand their fortunes.

There were many benefits for most delegates. Their ships could be protected by the nation's navy. A central government would create a common currency.

It also would regulate its value by promoting trade, both domestic and foreign. In addition, those who owned western lands could get protection from American Indians who resisted white settlement on their tribal lands.

Foundations of the American Constitution

Many of the delegates were well versed in the history, government, and political philosophy of ancient Greece and Rome, as well as that of their own time. They looked to leading thinkers in the field of government for guidance, including William Blackstone, the English jurist; Montesquieu, a famous French political philosopher; and British philosopher John Locke.

State Constitutions

Many ideas that were added to the U.S. Constitution were taken from the state constitutions that had been written during or soon after the American Revolution. A bicameral (two house) legislature was in existence in every state except Pennsylvania.

The provision that money bills had to originate in the lower house was taken almost word for word from the Massachusetts constitution of 1780. The impeachment process was adopted from similar provisions in the constitutions of Delaware, New Hampshire, and other states. The requirement that the Senate must approve executive appointments was suggested by New York's Council of Appointments.

Points of Agreement at the Convention

The delegates to the Philadelphia Convention agreed on several points: The Articles of Confederation were totally inadequate, and a new constitution had to be created if the nation hoped to survive and flourish. The national government should be stronger, but not so strong that the states would feel threatened by the loss of all their powers. Property rights must be protected.

The delegates believed in a limited democracy. Although they wanted the people to be represented, they feared giving too much power to the common people. They wanted to prevent anarchy (chaos), while also avoiding a dictatorship or monarchy. The Founding Fathers agreed that they wanted to create a republic where the ultimate power rested with the people. The people would be represented by chosen or elected delegates acting on their behalf.

Though they agreed on all these points, they also knew there would be many issues on which they would disagree. In order to create a successful new system of government, the convention delegates would have to compromise.

The Virginia Plan

No sooner had George Washington been chosen as the convention's presiding officer than Edmund Randolph rose to introduce fifteen resolutions, written by James Madison, on behalf of the Virginia delegates. These resolutions became known as the Virginia Plan. They contained some surprising proposals.

The Virginia Plan proposed almost a completely new form of government, one that differed dramatically from that of the Articles of Confederation. The delegates from Virginia proposed that the new government be a central one with power to make laws and to enforce them through its own executive and judicial branches. The plan also proposed that the Congress be bicameral. In it, the states would be represented on the basis of wealth and population. Larger states would

Edmund Randolph formally introduced the measures that became known as the Virginia Plan.

have more representatives. The Virginia delegates wanted this body to be given all the powers of the existing Congress. Also, this new government would have the authority "to legislate in all cases to which the separate States are incompetent, or in which the harmony of the United States may be interrupted by the exercise of individual Legislation. . . ."[1]

The New Jersey Plan

The convention spent the first two weeks discussing the Virginia Plan. As an alternative, William Patterson introduced the New Jersey Plan on July 14. It consisted of nine resolutions. The plan proposed that Congress be given the power to collect taxes and regulate commerce. Beyond that, New Jersey's proposal would not have significantly changed the Articles of Confederation.

Because New Jersey was a small state in terms of population, it wanted a one-chamber Congress. In it, all states would have equal weight. The New Jersey Plan also proposed a plural executive branch (made up of more than one person) to carry out the law, and a single national Supreme Court to supervise the interpretation of national laws by the state courts. Some of the New Jersey Plan proposals were used in the Constitution, but overall, the plan was rejected. The convention went back to discussing the Virginia Plan.

Debate Heats Up

Heated debates began. Some delegates even threatened to leave if their ideas were not adopted. The crucial issue was representation in the upper house of Congress. The issue deadlocked the convention.

Then, a committee was appointed. Eleven delegates would work together to come up with a

William Paterson of New Jersey proposed the New Jersey Plan, offered as an alternative to the ideas suggested by the Virginia delegation.

compromise. From this committee came what was to be known as the Connecticut Compromise, presented to the convention on July 5. It proposed that the upper house should have each state represented equally, with the condition that money bills originate only in the lower house.

The Problem of Slavery

One of the most contentious topics at the convention was the enslavement of blacks in America. Some Framers genuinely felt that the African-American slave was as much "man" as the white man. But this was a minority view. Southern delegates were uncompromising when it came to slavery—they needed to keep it going for the sake of the Southern economy. In fact, some of the Framers were also among the largest slave holders in the United States. Most Northern delegates did not like slavery, but for various reasons. Many feared allowing the black population in the South to grow would eventually hurt the North. They felt greater numbers of black slaves could lead to uprisings in the South and a march north to seek revenge on the people who bought the goods they had made or tended.

For some, slavery itself was at least tolerable, but the slave trade, the importation of new people from Africa, was not. Some simply opposed the idea of trafficking in human lives while others worried that importing more slaves would decrease the value of their surplus slaves in the slave market.

On June 11, Roger Sherman proposed representation be based on a count of all free men. The South wanted their slaves counted as whole persons, but that would never happen. James Wilson wanted to get past the slavery issue, and asked the Convention to adopt the same standard as that in the Articles: slaves would count as three-fifths persons. This issue returned on July 9, when some began to realize that the South could increase their representation in the Congress by simply importing new slaves. This concept alarmed many Northerners, and Northern states banded together on July 11 to completely remove slaves from the population counts.

In the end, both sides got something they wanted as a part of the Connecticut Compromise. Through a complicated bargain between Northern and Southern Framers, taxation and representation were tied together. The deal allowed the South to keep the three-fifths count for calculation of state levies, as long as they also had a three-fifths count for calculation of taxes.

The slave trade itself was debated hotly. The states of the deep south wanted it maintained; the North and the middle south were opposed. As the Convention progressed it became clear to the South and her allies that some compromise would be needed. In exchange for a prohibition on export taxes, the South agreed to allowing the slave trade to continue for just twenty more years, and for imported slaves to be taxable.

Though there were still other issues to be settled,

such as voting rights, federal courts, and election procedures, the delegates had overcome their most difficult hurdle. Over the next several weeks, their work continued.

Signing the Constitution

After four months of debate through a long, hot summer, the convention's work came to an end. They had a completed document to present to the nation. On September 17, 1787, the delegates met to take their seats for the last time in Philadelphia. George Washington, as presiding officer, called the meeting to order. The secretary read the final copy of the Constitution.

After it was read, the delegates signed the finished Constitution. Three prominent delegates—Elbridge Gerry, Edmund Randolph, and George Mason—were among those who refused to sign the completed document. They did not agree with certain provisions and would not sign unless the other delegates agreed to change the Constitution to suit them.[2] Among the delegates who did sign was Benjamin Franklin. As the eighty-one-year-old approached the table on which the Constitution sat he commented about the chair on which George Washington had sat throughout the Convention, which had a picture of a sun on its back. Franklin said: "I have often . . . in the course of this session . . . looked at that . . . without being able to tell whether it was rising or setting: but now at length I have the happiness to know that it is a rising and not a setting sun."[3]

After the signing was over, the delegates adjourned to the City Tavern to relax and celebrate their labors. Now they would face the task of getting the rest of the nation to approve of what they had done.

Ratification

After the Founding Fathers left Philadelphia, they faced the ordeal of convincing Congress and the states to approve the Constitution. Bitter arguments erupted over ratification. Ratification was to be carried out by conventions held in each of the states. At the conventions members would vote for or against the document.

Especially fierce was the debate in Virginia, New York, and Massachusetts.

The Constitutional Convention knew that unanimous consent would be almost impossible to get. So instead, the delegates made an agreement: when nine of the thirteen states had ratified the document, it would be accepted and a new government would be established.

Federalists Versus Anti-Federalists

Those who were in favor of the new Constitution and system of national government called themselves Federalists. The name emphasized the fact that, under the Constitution, the states would retain many of their powers but would be part of a national, or federal, government, too. In general, the Federalists represented wealthy property owners. They were supported by church and religious leaders and newspaper editors.

Those who opposed the new system of government were called Anti-Federalists. They found their support among the poorer people, especially small farmers who were burdened with terrible debt.

The battle over the Constitution seemed to be a division between the rich (Federalists) and the poor (Anti-Federalists). But the division was not clear. Sailors and working men in New York, Philadelphia, and Boston tended to support the Constitution. They hoped the new government would bring more trade and higher wages. Small farmers from the backcountry of Virginia also favored the Constitution and a new government because they wanted protection against the American Indians. The landed aristocracy of the Hudson Valley of New York, on the other hand, tended to oppose the Constitution for fear of heavy taxes if the federal government controlled taxes on imports.

The Federalists had a number of advantages in the ratification struggle. For one, they had a plan of government, whereas the Anti-Federalists could only criticize the Constitution without offering an alternative plan. Second, the Federalists were united, while the Anti-Federalist opposition was not as well organized. Third, the Anti-Federalists' districts were underrepresented, and many of the poorer people did not have the right to vote. At the time, the right to vote was restricted to property owners in many places, because politicians believed voters should have a responsible interest in casting their ballots. Fourth, although both sides had noteworthy personalities speaking out for their cause, the Federalists could boast of such famous men as George Washington, James Madison, Benjamin Franklin, John Jay, and

Alexander Hamilton, all of whom made powerful arguments supporting the Constitution.[1] Finally, the Federalists were both politically wise and shrewd. They were able to outmaneuver their opponents. For example, a convention to ratify the Constitution was quickly called in Pennsylvania before the Anti-Federalists could get organized.[2] Then, a slight majority opposing the Constitution in Massachusetts was turned around to a slight majority in favor of the Constitution when word was spread that popular local leader John Hancock might become the first vice president of the United States.[3]

Hamilton and The Federalist Papers

Hamilton's state of New York was one of the most important to win over because of its central location and large population. Hamilton had his hands full with the opposition and realized there was strong potential for rejection of the Constitution by his state. Therefore, he deliberately used his influence to delay the vote on ratification until he could gather more support.

With the help of James Madison and John Jay, Hamilton wrote a series of articles known as The Federalist Papers. Together, these essays tried to explain the strengths of the Constitution and the

Many people in Massachusetts agreed to accept the new Constitution because they hoped John Hancock, a popular local leader, would have a prominent position in the new government.

Alexander Hamilton used his great talents to help win ratification of the Constitution.

new national government. They quickly became the most important writings about the Constitution.

By the end of June 1788, ten states had ratified the Constitution. Hamilton was ready to ask for the vote in New York, arguing that the Constitution had been accepted by more than enough states, and it would seem unwise to be "left out" of the new nation. New York ratified the document and joined the Union.

Thus, by July 1788, all but two states—North Carolina and Rhode Island—had ratified the Constitution. Preparations began to start for the new government in 1789. These last two states finally ratified the Constitution, but not until after the inauguration of George Washington as the first president of the United States.

5

Concepts of the Constitution

The Constitution grants certain executive, legislative, and judicial powers to the national or central government, and it reserves to the states those powers not granted to the national government. Above all else, it makes the national government supreme by virtue of the Constitution being the supreme law of the land. Federal laws, as well as treaties entered into by the United States, are considered superior to state laws. They must be obeyed by all people and states. But the Constitution also denies certain powers to both the national and state governments, while others are given only to the national government and denied to state governments.

Powers of the Federal Government

The federal government exercises those powers that are specifically enumerated (listed) by the Constitution, as well as those powers that are implied (assumed, based on what is written) by those already enumerated. The states keep all powers not assigned to the federal government and not specifically denied to the states. The right of Congress to coin money and regulate its value is an enumerated power. Congress's right to establish a banking system, on the other hand, is an example of an implied power. It is allowed based on Congress's other enumerated powers, including the powers to coin money, to regulate interstate commerce, and to borrow money.

Control of education by the states is an example of a reserved power, one not given to the federal government, and therefore, kept for the states. In certain instances, the exercise of power may be concurrent (shared by both federal and state governments). For example, both the federal government and the states have the right to tax and to borrow money. In case of conflict between a federal law and a state law in an area of concurrent power, the federal law always takes first priority.

Exclusive powers are those that are reserved or granted only to the national government. Entering into treaty negotiations is an example of this kind of power. States may not make treaties with foreign nations.

Expressly limited powers are those denied by the Constitution to the national government. The power to tax exports, for example, is denied. There are certain implied limits on national power within the Constitution. States are considered the basic units of the federal system. Because the states are integral units of the United States, the national government may not use its powers to destroy the states or make it impossible for them to execute their own functions.

Powers Reserved to the States

The states have the power to collect taxes. The Constitution clarifies, however, that the states may not place a burden on the national government's efforts to collect taxes. States also have the power to regulate certain aspects of interstate commerce, as long as Congress does not believe such regulation oversteps Congress's own legal rights, and the Supreme Court believes the state action to be appropriate.

The states also have the power to take private property from their citizens for the good of the general public. They must, however, provide the owner of the property with due compensation (fair payment). The right of eminent domain, as this power is often called, is a concurrent power—one that also belongs to the federal government.

State power to regulate people and property is known as police power. States can pass laws to promote the public welfare of its citizens. There are constitutional limits placed on states in regard to their use of such power, however. Their actions must be consistent with the Constitution. In the event of questionable state action, the United States Supreme Court is the final judge.

Each state is free to establish its own form of government—as long as it is republican in form.

Interpretation and Conflict

In the well over two hundred years since the Constitution was adopted, conflicts have arisen over nation-state relationships. Simply put, these arguments are between those who emphasize states' rights and those who support a nationalist position.

States' rights advocates (supporters) claim that the Constitution is a compact, or contract, among the states. That is, it was the states that created the national government and gave it certain limited powers. States' rights supporters argue that, should there arise a question of whether a power belongs to the national government or to the states, that power should rest with the states. In this view, the powers of the national government are considered limited, and the Constitution is interpreted to avoid expanding its powers.

Supporters of the nationalist position deny that the national government was started by the states. They believe that the Constitution was created by the delegates of the Philadelphia Convention and comes from, as the Constitution's preamble states, "We the people of the United States." In their view, the national government was created directly by the people of the United States as a whole, not by the various state governments. Because the Constitution is the supreme law of the land, it cannot be less important than the laws of the states.

The eighteenth clause of section 8 of Article I of the Constitution is often called the "elastic clause." This clause is interpreted by so-called strict constructionists (those who wish to limit federal power) as allowing Congress to make only those laws that are "necessary and proper" to carry out the specific powers assigned to it. In this view, the federal government has the authority only to make laws that are absolutely necessary.

Loose constructionists, or those who support a liberal interpretation of the Constitution, believe the federal government has wider powers. They believe it can make laws when "necessary and proper" to carry out the powers assigned to it. The only limits of these powers are when the federal government's actions clearly conflict with the Constitution.

Separation of Powers and Checks and Balances

The powers of the national government are separated among the three branches. Congress has the power to

Public disapproval of the long war in Vietnam led to the passage of the War Powers Act in 1973, which limited the president's ability to make war without the consent of Congress.

make laws. The executive has the power to administer (carry out) the laws. And the judiciary has the authority to interpret and (with the aid of the executive) enforce the laws. In order to guard against too much growth in one branch of the government at the expense of the others, the authority of each department is restricted through an elaborate system of checks and balances.

The president may veto bills (reject proposed laws) passed by Congress. But this power is not absolute. Congress may override an executive veto by a two-thirds majority in each house. Similarly, the president's appointments to executive offices are subject to approval by a majority of the Senate. Treaties negotiated by the executive also need the approval of two thirds of the Senate to be valid (legal).

The president is Commander in Chief of the army and navy (supreme commander over all military forces), but the power to declare war lies with Congress. Over the years, presidents have personally delivered messages to the Congress to recommend that war be declared. However, Congress is responsible for actually deciding whether to declare war. The president, in the past, was able to send military forces anywhere, any time he or she pleased and engage in actual warfare without a formal declaration of war being made. This made many people worry that there was no way to check the war-making power of the president. After the United States became involved in the unpopular Korean and Vietnam wars, Congress, as a result of public outcry, decided to restrict the president's power. The War Powers Act of 1973 states that Congress will allow the president to engage in warfare without a congressional declaration of war for only up to sixty days (with a thirty-day period to remove troops). After that, the president must either withdraw the troops, ask Congress for an extension, or ask Congress to declare war. The act leaves the ultimate ability to make war with Congress.

The president is responsible for executing the laws. His or her assistants (the heads of the departments, or Cabinet members) may not participate with Congress in the enactment (creation) of legislation. There are times when laws passed by Congress and signed by the president may be set aside by the judiciary. The judicial branch could do so on the grounds of unconstitutionality (going against the Constitution). When this happens, Congress may submit a constitutional amendment to the states that would allow the

Abraham Lincoln was a strong president who used his constitutional powers fully, but he recognized the government's dependence on the consent of the people.

very power declared unconstitutional by the Supreme Court. If it is ratified, Congress will then have the power in question. However, this rarely happens.

Supremacy of the Constitution

The second paragraph of Article VI, proclaims the Constitution "the supreme Law of the Land." This paragraph involves accepting the doctrine of judicial review. Federal courts, in hearing cases, have the power to decide if federal laws conflict with the Constitution, or if a state's constitution or other statute interferes with federal law. In case of conflict, the judiciary has the power to declare laws null and void (not having legal power or force).

Amending the Constitution

The method of amending the Constitution was adopted by the Philadelphia Convention. Under the Constitution, amendments may be proposed by a two-thirds vote of both houses of Congress or by a national convention called by Congress when two-thirds of the state legislatures ask for one. Amendments become legal when they are ratified in three-fourths of the states, either by the state legislatures or by special conventions. One provision of the Constitution cannot be changed by the regular amending process.

Popular Sovereignty

This term means the government depends on the consent of the people it governs. This dependence on the will of the majority was defined by President Abraham Lincoln as "government of the people, by the people, for the people."[1]

Popular sovereignty did not, at first, mean democracy. However, the Constitution did create an environment that allowed the gradual development of political and social democracy. As the right to vote was extended to more people—such as African Americans and women—the tradition of giving the people the right to participate directly in shaping policy grew. Citizens can make their voices heard through public assembly (gathering), petitions, the press, personal letters, and other methods.

Equality of Citizens Before the Law

According to the Constitution, every American citizen must be provided with equality in a court of law. Each must be treated fairly. Citizens also have the right to campaign for and hold public office, as long as they qualify for the particular office. Congress cannot make laws to prevent certain people from exercising their rights.

Property Rights and Personal Liberties

The Constitution limits the powers of the nation and the states in order to protect individual citizens' property and liberty. Both Congress and the state legislatures are forbidden to pass bills of attainder—acts that punish a specific group of people without a trial. Ex post facto laws are also banned. These are laws passed that make an act committed before the law was passed a crime, or make the punishment for a crime more severe than it was at the time the crime was committed.

In the Bill of Rights, Congress may not interfere with freedom of religion, or take away freedom of speech or press or the right of assembly and petition. Other guarantees protect the individuals against unreasonable searches of the home or body. Seizure of property, unfair trials, excessive bail, or cruel and unusual punishment are forbidden. Citizens are also protected against being deprived of life, liberty, or property, without due process of law.

Implied Powers

Soon after the adoption of the Constitution, a conflict developed between two groups—those who wanted to preserve the rights of the states and the individuals, and those eager to extend federal power. The first group was made up of strict constructionists. They followed the beliefs of Thomas Jefferson. The second group consisted of loose constructionists. They believed in the ideals of Alexander Hamilton.

The states' rights champions, strict constructionists, believed the authority of the national government was limited to those powers actually written in the Constitution. The supporters of a stronger national government supported the idea of liberal interpretation. They used the so-called "elastic clause" to allow the federal government to take on powers that were not specifically granted by the Constitution but which could be considered necessary and proper for carrying out certain powers.

6

The Bill of Rights

The Bill of Rights—amendments one through ten—was added to the Constitution in 1791. The amendments were intended to end Anti-Federalists' criticism that the new Constitution did not sufficiently protect individual liberty. Even famous statesman Thomas Jefferson criticized the Constitution. He wrote to his friend James Madison that he liked the ideas in the document, but:

> I will now tell you what I do not like. First, the omission [lack] of a bill of rights, providing clearly . . . for freedom of religion, freedom of the press, protection against standing armies, restriction of monopolies, . . . and trials by jury. . . . [A] bill of rights is what the people are entitled to against every government on earth, general or particular, and what no just government should refuse. . . .[1]

Unlike Jefferson, many of the Founding Fathers opposed a Bill of Rights because it might appear to limit freedom by laying out specific rights. They feared it would imply that citizens had only those rights specifically mentioned and no others.

The Bill of Rights made no changes in any basic principle of the Constitution. This group of

James Madison, who played a big role in the drafting of the Constitution, is known as the Father of the Bill of Rights for his role in having the first ten amendments added.

amendments was added to the Constitution simply to provide additional insurance against the violation of liberties. The Bill of Rights, therefore, is often considered an integral part of the original Constitution rather than an addition that came about due to changing times.

To create the Bill of Rights, Founding Father James Madison, who is known as the Father of the Bill of Rights, took many suggestions from those who believed personal liberties needed protection in the Constitution. After reviewing them, he condensed these ideas and presented them to the House of Representatives on June 8, 1789.[2] Congress approved twelve of the suggested amendments and forwarded these to the states for ratification. At the end of a two-year period, the states accepted ten of Madison's twelve. The ten amendments went into effect in 1791 as the Bill of Rights.

First Amendment: Freedom of Opinion

The First Amendment guarantees freedom of religion, speech, press, assembly, and petition. It assures citizens that the federal government shall not restrict freedom of worship. It specifically prohibits Congress from establishing an official, government-supported church. Under the First Amendment, the federal government cannot require citizens to pay taxes to support a certain church, nor can people be prohibited from worshipping in any way they see fit. However, if a certain religion recommends a practice that is contrary to public morals, such as polygamy (marriage to more than one spouse), Congress may prohibit such a practice.

The freedom of speech and press refer to the right of citizens to say or publish what they choose. This freedom, however, has been restrained during periods of emergency, when the government felt it might be dangerous to allow opinions that might hurt the nation if publicized. Even under normal conditions, free speech and press can violate federal laws, such as when obscene literature is sent through the mail. The only people who may say whatever they please without fear of punishment under the law are members of Congress on the floor of their respective houses while in session. As a general rule, a person may say anything that is not libelous or slanderous (wrongly injuring the character or reputation of another person) and as long as it does not encourage the violent overthrow of the government.

The principles governing freedom of speech also affect freedom of the press. There is no government censorship of the press in the United States. In time of war, however, the principles of free speech and press are often modified for the protection of the country.

The people of the United States also have the right to assemble peaceably under the First Amendment. The only restriction comes from the word peaceably. Assembly may not be prevented, as long as the proper authorities have "reasonable" assurance that the meeting will be peaceful.

The ability to petition the government is highly prized by all free people. In the United States, anyone may appeal to the federal government or the government of a state to complain about issues or policies with which he or she disagrees. The right to petition carries with it the right to be heard. However, being heard and having something done to resolve the complaint are quite different. Just because citizens express themselves does not mean that the government will listen and make changes.

Second Amendment: The Right to Bear Arms

"The right of the people to keep and bear Arms" is a controversial one. It refers to keeping weapons for the purposes of protecting the community. The conditions under which an individual person may obtain, possess, carry, and use weapons is almost entirely under the control of the states.

The Second Amendment aims to prevent Congress from interfering with the right of the states to maintain militias (private armies). It does not, however, prevent the states from regulating the possession and use of firearms and other weapons. Such regulation usually takes the form of a licensing system, which is considered an exercise of a state's police power.

The Second Amendment prevents the government from seizing all weapons in a certain state or district, or throughout the entire country, in order to leave the people helpless. The article does not necessarily mean that a state cannot regulate the sale and display of firearms. Such laws are not generally considered infringements of the right to bear arms. Firearms, however, are often used for recreational activities such as hunting and target shooting. For this reason, many gun enthusiasts protest Congress's and states' attempts to make strict regulations for firearms ownership and use.

Third Amendment: Quartering Troops

In the eighteenth century, it was common for the British government to lodge soldiers in private homes, regardless of the homeowners' wishes. This was a source of annoyance between the American colonists and the British government and was even mentioned in the Declaration of Independence.

Traditionally, soldiers have been quartered in private houses during peacetime for two reasons: to make a person the authorities wished to punish, uncomfortable or to extort money from a person. If the government wanted to ruin someone financially, it could keep a company of soldiers in his or her house. If, on the other hand, the authorities needed money, they could assign a company of soldiers to someone's house and then withdraw the company only after a certain sum was paid. This was blackmail, pure and simple.

The quartering of troops was one of the causes of the American Revolution. The Founding Fathers did not want it to occur again.

Fourth Amendment: Searches and Seizures

The Fourth Amendment guarantees the security of persons and their homes against unreasonable searches and seizures. This provision is a reminder of the struggle the American colonists fought against the writs of assistance—general search warrants issued during the colonial period. These writs, issued to control smuggling, allowed a search of any premises without specifically stating an address, a person's name, or reason for the search. Under the Constitution, a person's home or belongings cannot be searched unless officers have a specific search warrant. Only the place mentioned in the warrant may be searched, and a search may be made only for the items described in the warrant.

There are some exceptions. For example, a person may not commit a murder and defy arrest by hiding out in a certain house until a warrant can be obtained. However, in every case of arrest or seizure without a warrant, the burden of proof—that the case is one of necessity—is on the officer who makes the arrest or seizure.

In 1985, the Supreme Court made a ruling in *New Jersey* v. *T.L.O.* about search and seizure of student property in public schools. The Court decided that school officials may search students' bodies, purses, or book bags if they have "reasonable" belief that there has been a violation of school rules or the law.[3] The Court's decision does not allow random searches of students, but it does not hold school officials to the same strict standards police have to follow when they obtain search warrants for suspects.

Fifth Amendment: Rights of Accused Persons

The Fifth Amendment protects the rights of people accused of crimes. In capital crimes (punishable by death), and in lesser crimes punishable by imprisonment, the accused may not be held for trial unless indicted (formally charged) by a grand jury. This grand jury decides whether or not the evidence is enough to hold the accused for trial. If so, the grand jury has an indictment issued.

Indictment does not mean that the accused is guilty. It merely means that the grand jury believes the accused should be tried before a judge and a trial jury (petit jury). The grand jury gives its decision by a majority vote. The grand jury's job is to protect an innocent person from undergoing the hardships and losses a trial entails. The grand jury also saves the state the time and expense of trying suspects in cases without enough evidence to convict.

The innocence or guilt of the accused is determined by a petit jury, usually made up of twelve members. Generally, a unanimous verdict (decision) is needed to convict or acquit. The trial must be public and must take place in the state or district where the crime was committed.

A person accused of a crime, who has been acquitted by a unanimous verdict of a petit jury, may never be tried again for that particular crime involving the same people, time, and place. To try someone twice for the same crime would be to place the accused in danger twice (double jeopardy). That is illegal.

In the past, accused persons had been forced to testify in cases about themselves. Often, torture was used to get them to confess their guilt. The Fifth Amendment provides that no person can be forced to be a witness against him- or herself. In addition, according to judicial practice, a husband cannot be forced to testify against his wife, nor the wife against the husband. This is called a "privilege." Of course, the accused still has the right to testify if he or she chooses to do so. The point of the amendment is that a person does not have to testify in any way that might show his or her guilt.

The Fifth Amendment says that no person shall be deprived of life, liberty, or property without due process of law. This provision protects citizens against arbitrary acts by those in authority. Often, the government—municipal, state, or federal—takes private property for public uses. For instance, land might be taken to build a road, playground, railroad, or military installation. This is known as the government's right of eminent domain. Under the Fifth Amendment, the government must provide just compensation (fair payment) to property owners when it exercises this right. If the people who own the property and the government are not able to agree on a price, the courts determine what price is fair.

Sixth Amendment: More Rights of Accused Persons

The Sixth Amendment also deals with the rights of people accused of crimes. A speedy trial is guaranteed. Although crowded courts may delay trials, every effort must be made to handle the case in a timely manner. In the past, suspects were sometimes held in prison for many years without trial. Governments often held the accused deliberately to punish them or to keep them from speaking out against the government. The Sixth Amendment seeks to prevent such unfair treatment.

Except in certain cases involving public morals, trials must be public. The jury is chosen from the state and district where the crime was committed. If the accused feels that the people of the district where the crime was committed are prejudiced because of extensive pre-trial media coverage, he or she may ask for the trial to be moved to another district. This is called a change of venue.

The accused must be informed of the specific charges against him or her, in order to prepare a defense. In court, the witnesses against the suspect may not whisper their accusations secretly to the judge. They must confront the accused openly.

The accused has the same right as the state to call witnesses to testify. If he or she cannot afford a lawyer, the state must assign counsel for the defense in felony (serious) cases.

The Constitution is designed to give those charged with crimes every possible chance to prove their innocence. This comes from the theory embraced by the Founders that it is better to let ten guilty people go free than to punish one innocent person.

Seventh Amendment: Suits at Common Law

A civil suit at common law is a dispute in which property or personal damages are involved. Common law is based on established customs and court decisions rather than written law. The principles of common law come from the colonial period, when the states were colonies of the British Empire. For instance, under common law, if a certain path or road was used by the public without restrictions, in the absence of any law to the contrary, after a certain period of years that road became a public highway.

Two principles of common law allow for a case tried by a jury to be reexamined. In the first case, the court where the case was tried may order a new trial. In the second case, a higher court may on a writ of error review the law, but not the facts, in the case.

Eighth Amendment: Bails and Punishments

On the principle that a person is innocent until proven guilty, it is customary to allow accused persons their liberty. This happens only after the court has demanded a property guarantee that the accused person will appear for trial. The Eighth Amendment guarantees that the amount of bail must be fixed according to the seriousness of the charge. In certain cases, such as murders, it may be refused altogether.

The Eighth Amendment protects against cruel and unusual punishment, but only in criminal sanctions. Originally designed to prevent suspects or convicted criminals from being tortured, the amendment raises some issues that remain controversial even today, such as whether the death penalty can be considered cruel and unusual.

Ninth Amendment: Rights Not Enumerated

This amendment states that the people have certain rights, even if they are not specifically written into the Constitution. The fact that a certain right is not clearly mentioned in the Constitution does not mean that the people do not have this right. If a right is not defined in the Constitution, in the absence of laws to the contrary, that right is assumed to be held by the people.

Tenth Amendment: Powers Not Delegated

The last amendment of the Bill of Rights states the central point of the federal system: The federal government holds only those powers given to it or implied by the Constitution. All other powers, except those expressly denied to the states, are reserved to the states, or to the people. This theory forms the basis of the doctrine of states' rights. The main idea of this amendment is to protect the states from an overextension of federal power.

Adjustment and Extension of Rights

Great changes have taken place since the ratification of the United States Constitution in 1788. The law has changed with the times and has grown with the nation. Its meaning has been altered, expanded, and added to, most clearly with the acceptance of formal amendments.

Adjustments in the Machinery of the Government

The Bill of Rights was added to the Constitution to protect the rights of individual citizens. Some constitutional amendments, however, brought about practical improvements and minor adjustments in the way the federal government works.

The Eleventh Amendment: Suits Against States

The Eleventh Amendment was adopted in 1795 as a concession to states' rights. It declares that a state may not be sued in the federal courts by a citizen of another state or of a foreign country.

Shortly after the Constitution went into effect, states found themselves being sued by private individuals in federal courts. The Eleventh Amendment grew out of the case of *Chisholm* v. *Georgia* (1793). In this case, the Supreme Court ruled that the state of Georgia could be sued by a citizen of another state in a federal court. The Supreme Court upheld a decision in which the state of Georgia was ordered to pay damages to the heirs of a British subject whose property had been taken during the American Revolution.[1]

This decision caused such an outcry of protest that Congress proposed the Eleventh Amendment to forbid individuals from suing states in federal courts. The Eleventh Amendment, adopted in 1795, took away from the federal courts the legal right, or jurisdiction, over suits against states that are started by citizens of other states or foreign countries. It is, however, possible to bring suit against a state (or its officers) in the state's own courts if the state gives its consent.

The Eleventh Amendment does not prevent a state from being sued by another state or foreign country. In these instances, the suit is tried in a federal district court or in the United States Supreme Court.

The Twelfth Amendment: Presidential Elections

The Twelfth Amendment, adopted in 1804, changed the way presidents were elected. The original method of election, contained in the Constitution, was to cast votes for the president only. The candidate with the most votes became president, while the person with the next most votes became vice president.

The development of political parties made this method of election unworkable. In some cases, people from opposing parties were elected to serve together as president and vice president. For example, in 1796,

Because of the way the Constitution set up presidential elections in the early years of the American republic, Federalist John Adams (seen here) had Democratic-Republican Thomas Jefferson as his vice president.

Federalist John Adams became president, while Democratic-Republican Thomas Jefferson became vice president. Then, in the election of 1800, Thomas Jefferson and Aaron Burr, candidates of the Democratic-Republican party, each received seventy-three electoral votes. The Constitution provided that, in the event of a tie, the election would be decided by the House of Representatives. Each state, regardless of the number of representatives it had, would get one vote. A severe political battle ensued. In the end, Jefferson was elected president by the House of Representatives.

To prevent such cases from happening again, the Twelfth Amendment was adopted. It states that there are to be separate ballots for president and vice president. In the event of a tie, or if no candidate wins a majority, the House of Representatives shall select the president by voting for one of the three candidates who received the highest number of electoral votes. The Senate chooses the vice president.

In 1824, the electoral vote was distributed among four candidates; no candidate received a majority of the total. The House then elected John Quincy Adams, by the process outlined in the Twelfth Amendment.

A majority of electoral votes is also needed for the

John Quincy Adams, son of second president John Adams, was elected president by a vote in the House of Representatives.

election of the vice president. In the event that no candidate receives a majority, the Senate will select the vice president from the two candidates who have the highest number of votes. A majority of the Senate's entire membership is necessary to make a choice.

The last sentence of the amendment provides that the qualifications for the vice presidency shall be the same as for the presidency. This provision was not necessary under the original method of election. Because the electors cast their ballots only for president, every candidate had to meet the qualifications for president.

American citizens voting in a presidential election are actually voting for electors, who will later cast their votes in the Electoral College. These electors are pledged, or expected, to vote in line with the people's choices. In 1948, an unpledged presidential elector in Tennessee used his constitutional right to vote for whom he pleased. Instead of voting for the Democratic candidate as expected, he cast his ballot for the nominee of the States' Rights party, J. Strom Thurmond.

The Supreme Court ruled in 1952 that a political party could legally require a binding pledge that an elector vote for the party nominee. Despite this, an Alabama elector who was pledged to Adlai Stevenson in the 1956 election voted for a local judge who had never even been nominated for the presidency, and Congress accepted it. Although such cases are rare, there is always the possibility that electors will ignore the popular vote and cast their ballots for whomever they wish.

The Twentieth Amendment: Terms of Office

Approved in 1933, the Twentieth Amendment made a logical and much-needed adjustment in the sessions of Congress. The new system virtually eliminated the lame duck session, during which the outgoing Congress—many of whom were "lame ducks," who had failed to be reelected—met before the newly elected Congress was sworn in. The amendment moved up the date at which the new Congress would be sworn in, thereby shortening the length of time during which Congress was run by "lame ducks."

By providing for the president's inauguration to take place on January 20 instead of March 4, the Twentieth Amendment also reduced the waiting period between the time a new president is elected and the time he takes office.

Section 3 of the amendment states that Congress may make a law to provide for possible deaths of the president-elect and vice president-elect before they are sworn in. Congress has passed laws to arrange for presidential succession in the event of the death of both the president and vice president. In 1947, an act was passed stating that the office of president would pass to the speaker of the House of Representatives if both the president and vice president have died. The next in line is the president pro tempore of the Senate (the senator who presides over the Senate in the absence of the vice president). The presidential succession then goes in the following order: secretary of state; secretary of the treasury; secretary of defense; attorney general; secretary of the interior; secretary of agriculture; secretary of commerce; secretary of labor; secretary of health, education, and welfare; secretary of housing and urban development; secretary of transportation; secretary of energy; secretary of education; and secretary of veterans' affairs.

The Twentieth Amendment is at times referred to as the "Norris Amendment" because it was Senator

Franklin Delano Roosevelt was the only president to be elected four times.

George William Norris of Nebraska who led the fight to have it adopted.

The Twenty-second Amendment: Term Limits

The Twenty-second Amendment, ratified in 1951, limits a president to two consecutive terms, or to one term if he or she has served more than two years of his predecessor's term. The president may not serve more than a total of ten consecutive years. On the other hand he or she may leave office, run, and serve again.

Limiting a president to two terms was tradition until 1940, when the custom was shattered by the election of Franklin D. Roosevelt to a third term. Earlier presidents had served no more than two terms, following the example set by George Washington. In 1944, when Roosevelt was elected to a fourth term, many feared it set a dangerous precedent.

In 1947, two years after Roosevelt's death (during his fourth term), Congress proposed a constitutional amendment limiting presidential tenure. By February 1951, the necessary thirty-six states had ratified the proposal. As a matter of official courtesy, the new amendment did not apply to the president in office at the time of its ratification (Harry Truman). Early in 1952, however, Truman declined to run again. President Dwight Eisenhower became the first president subject to the new amendment.

The Twenty-third Amendment: Voting in Washington, D.C.

The Twenty-third Amendment, adopted in 1961, gives the people of the District of Columbia three votes in the Electoral College that chooses the president and vice president. The number of electoral votes each state has is equal to the number of representatives it has in the House of Representatives plus its two senators. Because Washington, D.C., has no voting representatives in Congress, before the Twenty-third Amendment, it had no electors in the Electoral College either.

President John F. Kennedy urged Congress to take action to give the residents of the District of Columbia home rule. Following many years of agitation, Congress finally agreed that residents of the nation's capital are entitled to a voice (if only a partial one) in national politics.

So in June 1960, Congress submitted to the states a proposed amendment giving the District of Columbia three electoral votes in the election of the president and vice president. By March 1961, the amendment was ratified.

The Extension of Democracy

A third group of amendments restricts the powers of the states in order to protect and promote liberty and democracy. These amendments, which grew out of the Civil War and various reform movements, were designed chiefly to extend political rights to groups of people, including African Americans and women, who had not been considered full citizens earlier.

The Thirteenth Amendment: Abolition of Slavery

This amendment represented the final act of ending slavery in the United States. Although some slaves had been freed earlier by various means, the question of a constitutional amendment abolishing slavery was a major issue in the presidential campaign of 1864, which took place during the Civil War. In this election, Lincoln was reelected by a large majority (because the Southern Confederate states were not permitted electors). The amendment was proposed by the necessary two-thirds of both Houses of Congress in January 1865. Ratification of the amendment became one of the requirements for reentry to the Union. By the end of that year, three-fourths of the state legislatures had ratified it and the amendment was declared in force.

The Thirteenth Amendment became an issue in later years. During World War I, conscription (the draft) was used. Some people protested, claiming the draft was a form of "involuntary servitude" and, therefore, a violation of the Thirteenth Amendment. The Supreme Court ruled, however, that the federal government had the right to draft soldiers into the military service through its power to raise and support armies.

The Fourteenth Amendment: Limitations on State Action

African-American slaves were freed by the Thirteenth Amendment. The Fourteenth made them citizens.

The Fourteenth Amendment was designed to prevent the former slaves from having their rights restricted. In the South after the Civil War, many white Southerners were opposed to the idea of having to live in an equal society with the African Americans who were once their slaves. As a result, Southern lawmakers tried to limit the rights of the former slaves in any way possible.

The Fourteenth Amendment grew out of the determination of the Radical Republicans in Congress to safeguard the rights of the newly freed African Americans and to punish the leaders of the

After the Civil War, racist white groups banded together to try to prevent African Americans from exercising their newly won civil rights.

Confederacy (the South during the Civil War). They wanted the amendment to emphasize the fact that African Americans are citizens.

In one sense, the Fourteenth Amendment showed the reaction of the Northern states to laws many of the Southern states had passed after the adoption of the Thirteenth Amendment. These laws, called "black codes," were designed to put African Americans on a lower social and economic level than their fellow citizens. The Fourteenth Amendment, adopted in 1868, clearly defined citizenship for the first time and strongly stated that state citizenship and United States citizenship are distinct.

At first, it seemed that the amendment's sweeping language, ensuring that "immunities and privileges" would be protected, would give the federal government complete power to regulate the business and civil rights of the people of every state. But in the famous *Slaughter-House Cases* of 1873, the Supreme Court ruled that a citizen's rights come either from the federal Constitution and laws or from state constitutions and laws. If founded on state laws, the citizen must look to the state, not the federal government, for protection. The Fourteenth Amendment, the Court said, was not meant to "degrade the State governments by subjecting them to the control of Congress. . . ."[2] Again, in the *Civil Rights Cases* of 1883, the Supreme Court ruled that while the equal protection of the Fourteenth Amendment prevented a state from discriminating between "colored" persons and white persons, Congress could not prevent individuals, such as innkeepers, from such discrimination. According to the Court, "Individual invasion of individual rights is not the subject matter of the amendment."[3] Since 1890, however, the Supreme Court has held that the word person includes corporations. Railroads, public utilities, and corporations in general have successfully appealed to the Supreme Court when states have passed laws they believed deprived them of liberty or property. The Civil Rights Act of 1964 prohibited discrimination in public accommodations.

The due process clause was made a part of the Fourteenth Amendment in order to prevent the states from depriving African Americans of life, liberty, or property except through legal court procedures. This clause has probably aroused more controversy than any other phrase in the Constitution. Its interpretation has been gradually broadened over the years. It now offers protection against arbitrary or unreasonable regulation of private rights. In general, the Supreme Court has held that a state may not unduly restrict liberty, or property, unless such restriction is either a necessary exercise of its police power or a temporary emergency measure.

Section 2 of the Fourteenth Amendment specifically abolished the Three-fifths Ratio in determining representation and direct taxes. The Fourteenth Amendment made clear that African Americans were to be counted as people, just the same as whites.

In order to prevent the states from discriminating against certain groups of citizens, the Fourteenth Amendment declares that any state that denies the right to vote to qualified citizens, shall have its representation in Congress reduced. This section has never been enforced. Congress itself had little faith in this provision. In fact, just six months after the ratification of the Fourteenth Amendment, Congress proposed the Fifteenth Amendment to deal specifically with the right to vote.

Other provisions of the Fourteenth Amendment deal with excluding certain former Confederates from federal offices. At the time, this ruled out practically the entire white population of the South who had had experience in government affairs. Congress hoped to protect the former slaves' newly won rights by preventing Confederates from entering public service and passing laws to hurt them. Over time, Congress removed these restrictions. By 1898, all were gone.

After the Civil War, many African Americans voted for the first time. Unfortunately, after troops were removed from the South at the end of Reconstruction, most African Americans would no longer be willing to risk their lives to exercise their voting rights.

At first, Congress relied on military occupation to enforce the Fourteenth Amendment. White Southern public opinion, however, was overwhelmingly opposed to accepting African Americans as full social and political equals. By various methods, ranging from persuasion to intimidation and violence, whites tried to frighten African Americans away from the polls and prevent them from exercising their new political rights. Although many African Americans worked hard to end such treatment, it was not until the civil rights movement of the twentieth century that African Americans would make real progress toward achieving political equality in the Southern states.

The Fifteenth Amendment: African-American Suffrage

The Fifteenth Amendment was proposed to give former slaves further protection from Southern politicians who hoped to keep them from exercising their rights. The amendment forbids the states to take away the right to vote because of race. However, this amendment does not force the states to give the vote to everyone. The states may deny the right to vote to any citizen based on qualifications they determine, so long as it is not because of race, color, or previous condition of servitude (slavery).

The amendment leaves the states with a great deal of authority. For instance, the Constitution does not forbid the states to establish voting qualifications based on age, literacy, length of residence, or payment of taxes.

For a long time, Southern states were able to successfully prevent African Americans from voting, despite the Fifteenth Amendment. They did this by setting up poll taxes (a tax a person paid in order to vote), literacy tests (determining one's ability to read and interpret), and other devices.

The Supreme Court judged some of these invalid, and others were outmoded over the years. Only through laws passed as a result of the civil rights movement did African Americans finally begin to win full voting rights in the 1950s and 1960s.

The Seventeenth Amendment: Direct Election of Senators

The Seventeenth Amendment, adopted in 1913, states that United States senators shall be elected by the people of each state (direct election) rather than by the state legislatures (indirect election). It took many years after its proposal for this amendment to finally pass. The idea behind it was to make choosing senators more democratic, to reduce corruption, and improve state government. Often, state legislatures had been influenced in their selection of senators by bribery or by powerful political leaders called bosses. Many people also came to believe that the role of a legislature should be to make laws for the good of the state, not to choose federal officials.

The original provision of the Constitution that senators were to be chosen by state legislatures was designed, in part at least, to make the upper house of Congress a check on the popularly elected House of Representatives. With the growth of democratic sentiment during the nineteenth century, however, agitation for popular election of senators increased. In 1904, Oregon established the precedent of permitting voters to indicate their choice for United States senators while casting their ballots for members of the state legislature. By 1911, this system of senatorial preference had been adopted by more than three fourths of the states. Congress proposed the Seventeenth Amendment, which was ratified in 1913, due to the influence of public opinion.

The Nineteenth Amendment: Women's Suffrage

The Nineteenth Amendment, approved in 1920, forbade any state to deny the right to vote on account of sex. It is interesting to note that the men of Congress granted the right to vote to adult African-American males (former slaves) in 1870, but continued to deny that very same right to white women who had already been considered citizens of the United States.

The Nineteenth Amendment marked one of the ultimate triumphs of the reform movements that had started to sweep America during the nineteenth century. The women's rights movement, dating from the first women's rights convention in Seneca Falls, New York, in 1848, had struggled for years to win equal political rights for women. Women had gained full suffrage rights in four western states (Wyoming, Colorado, Utah, and Idaho) before 1900. However, because the states determined voting qualifications, women throughout the country could not easily win the right to vote without a national constitutional amendment. About twenty states had passed equal suffrage laws when the Nineteenth Amendment was finally ratified by the necessary two thirds of both Houses of Congress in June 1919. The thirty-sixth state, Tennessee, ratified the amendment on August 28, 1920. This amendment does not take away the right to determine the qualifications of voters from the states. It simply forbids the states to make any distinction on account of sex.

Extension of the Power of the Federal Government

Other amendments passed over the years gave additional power to the federal government.

After decades of struggling to win the right to vote, the women's suffrage movement finally won success with the ratification of the Nineteenth Amendment in 1920.

The Sixteenth Amendment

The Sixteenth Amendment, adopted in 1913, gives Congress the power to levy taxes on what people earn without apportioning (dividing) such taxes among the states according to population.

During the Civil War, Congress had imposed an income tax as a war measure. But when Congress tried to charge an income tax during peacetime, the Supreme Court declared the measure unconstitutional. Not until 1913 were the supporters of a federal income tax able to secure the adoption of an amendment to the Constitution, giving Congress the power to tax incomes without apportioning.

The Eighteenth Amendment: Prohibition

The Eighteenth Amendment, approved in 1919, provided for federal-state enforcement of nationwide prohibition, making alcoholic beverages illegal. This was an innovation because it gave the federal government control over one aspect of the personal habits of individuals.

Except for slavery, no moral issue in United States history has aroused more political controversy. In 1846, Maine became the first state to prohibit the manufacture and sale of alcoholic beverages. By 1916, twenty-four states had passed statewide prohibition laws. Nearly all the others had legalized some form of local option, which allowed towns and cities within the state to decide whether or not to prohibit the sale of liquor.

World War I provided unexpected assistance to the movement to outlaw alcoholic beverages. In order to conserve grain, Congress passed two wartime prohibition measures. At the same time, it placed before the states a National Prohibition Amendment, which was adopted in January 1919. Prohibition went into effect one year later.

In order to enforce the Eighteenth Amendment, Congress passed the Volstead Act. This law defined intoxicating liquor as any beverage containing one half of one percent or more of alcohol.

The Eighteenth Amendment has the distinction of being the only amendment to be repealed (overruled) by later action. The amendment proved almost impossible to uphold and enforce fully. In December 1933, national prohibition was repealed by the Twenty-first Amendment.

Other Amendments

In addition to the amendments that broadened the powers of government, outlined individual liberties, and expanded citizenship, some amendments have been added to the Constitution to deal with specific issues that have arisen over time.

Twenty-fourth Amendment: Anti-Poll Tax

As a means of discouraging African Americans from voting after the Civil War and even into the twentieth century, some places, especially in the South, required a tax to be paid in order to vote. Because most former slaves were too poor to pay, they were easily excluded from the political process. During the civil rights movement, African Americans made strong protests of such unfair laws and demanded that their constitutional rights be recognized. The Twenty-fourth Amendment, ratified in 1964, was one of many measures taken to help secure the rights of African Americans. It outlawed the use of poll taxes, taking away some of the states' discretion to decide what qualifications must be met to vote. This amendment, however, applies only to the national elections. The states may still decide what qualifies a voter in statewide elections.

The Twenty-fifth Amendment: Presidential Succession Act

This amendment clarifies Article I, Section 1, Clause 6, which states that the vice president becomes president on the death, resignation, or removal of the president from office. In such cases, the vice president is sworn in to officially become president.

Should the president be unable to carry out the duties of the office, he or she must give notice of this in writing to Congress or to the vice president and a majority of the Cabinet. In this instance, the vice president becomes acting president until the president is again able to function. At that point, the president must once again inform Congress in writing.

The president may be denied the right to resume office if the vice president and a majority of department heads of the Cabinet send a written statement to Congress saying that the president is not able to carry out the duties of office. Congress then must meet within forty-eight hours (if it is not in session). Congress has twenty-one days after receiving the written statement to determine a course of action, which must be approved by a two-thirds vote in each house.

Two vice presidents have resigned from office through United States history. John C. Calhoun resigned on December 28, 1832, three months before the expiration of his term, to become a senator for South Carolina. Spiro T. Agnew resigned on October 10, 1973, after pleading no contest to a charge of federal income tax evasion. When Agnew resigned, President Richard Nixon nominated Gerald Ford, the minority leader of the House, to fill the vice-presidential vacancy. The Senate and House approved the nomination and Ford was sworn in on December 6, 1973. Less than a year later, in August 1974, Ford became president when Richard Nixon became the first president to resign. On August 20, 1974, Ford nominated Nelson Rockefeller to be vice president. He was confirmed and sworn in on December 10, 1974. In less than one year, two occasions had arisen for using the provisions of the Twenty-fifth Amendment to fill a vacancy in the vice presidency. And, for the only time in the history of the country, the United States had a president who was neither nominated nor elected by the people.

Twenty-sixth Amendment: Voting Age Lowered

During the 1960s, the United States became involved in an unpopular war in Vietnam. Many of those who expressed the strongest opposition to the war were

Partly because so many young people were both fighting in the war in Vietnam and making their voices heard in opposition to it, the Twenty-sixth Amendment to lower the voting age won great support.

young people—teenagers and college students. Some of these antiwar activists protested the apparent injustice of drafting young men from the ages of eighteen to twenty to fight in the military, when citizens in most states had to be twenty-one to vote. It seemed wrong that people would be allowed to fight for their country without being allowed a voice in its political affairs. In response to this agitation, Congress passed the Twenty-sixth Amendment on March 23, 1971. Ratified on July 1, 1971, the amendment lowered the minimum voting age to eighteen.

Twenty-seventh Amendment: Congressional Salaries

The most recent amendment to be added to the United States Constitution is, in some ways, the most curious. It provides that, if Congress votes itself a pay raise, that raise cannot go into effect until after an election takes place. The idea is to allow citizens to express their disapproval of the pay raise by voting those who passed it out of office, and preventing them from enjoying its benefits. What is most interesting about the amendment is that it was first proposed as part of James Madison's suggested Bill of Rights, in September 1789. It was finally ratified by the vote of Michigan on May 7, 1992.[4]

Failed Amendments

Unlike the Twenty-seventh Amendment, which was added to the Constitution after a delay of over two hundred years, there have been some amendments that failed altogether. Among these are amendments that would prohibit flag burning as a sign of political protest. Perhaps the best known, however, is the famous Equal Rights Amendment.

The Equal Rights Amendment (ERA) was first submitted for ratification in 1972. It was a product of the growing movement for equal rights for women in American society. Although women enjoyed the right to vote and were supposed to be equal to men under the law, many women felt they faced discrimination on account of sex in the job market. In fact, women were generally paid less money than men for doing the same jobs.

The purpose of the ERA was to prevent discrimination toward women in any way, just as the Thirteenth, Fourteenth, and Fifteenth amendments were added to the Constitution to prevent discrimination against African Americans. First introduced in Congress in 1923, the amendment was passed by Congress in 1972, but had a time limit of seven years for ratification.[5] In 1978, Congress extended the deadline until June 30, 1982. Still, by that time, only thirty-five of the needed thirty-eight states had ratified the amendment, and the amendment was shelved. Congress has reintroduced the ERA several times, but so far, it has not been passed.

8

The Constitution at Work

Since its adoption in 1789, the United States Constitution has gone through many changes. For the most part, though, it has worked in the way its framers intended—to protect the individual rights of American citizens and to establish a government that would function smoothly and provide for peaceful transfers of power through elections.

Over the years, Congress has proposed many amendments to the Constitution. Some of these have increased the power of the federal government, to the detriment of the states. However, as time went by and the nation suffered through several crises, including the Civil War, two world wars, and the Great Depression, it became clear that the federal government needed to play a bigger role in American society. Although its powers were limited by the Constitution, amendment and interpretation have increased the role of the federal government. More liberal views of the Constitution have allowed the federal government to take on the task of extending aid to the poor and providing Social Security benefits to working Americans.

As the United States' population increased and more groups of people, such as African Americans and women, won their rights to be considered citizens and to vote, the Constitution has allowed for the expansion of liberty to include these individuals. The amendment process has also made America a more direct democracy, allowing for direct election of senators and treating the Electoral College almost as a rubber stamp that echoes the vote of the people. Over time, the American government has moved away from the Founding Fathers' vision of a republic led by an elite group of well-educated men like themselves and toward a democracy in which all citizens have a voice in the policies that affect their lives. These sweeping changes have all come about through the machinery of the Constitution, created by a group of influential men during the hot summer of 1787.

Throughout the course of its history, the Constitution has been interpreted differently by different people, based on their own views of the appropriate amount of power that should be held by the states or the federal government. At times, the Constitution has led to terrible disagreement, and even to the Civil War. But in the end, the Constitution has stood the test of time, and will continue to provide American citizens with the security of knowing that their rights are protected.

THE CONSTITUTION OF THE UNITED STATES

The text of the Constitution is presented here. All words are given their modern spelling and capitalization. Brackets [ ] indicate parts that have been changed or set aside by amendments.

Preamble

We the People of the United States, in Order to form a more perfect Union, establish Justice, insure domestic Tranquillity, provide for the common defence, promote the general Welfare, and secure the Blessings of Liberty to ourselves and our Posterity, do ordain and establish this Constitution for the United States of America.

ARTICLE I

The Legislative Branch

Section 1. All legislative powers herein granted shall be vested in a Congress of the United States, which shall consist of a Senate and House of Representatives.

The House of Representatives

Section 2. (1) The House of Representatives shall be composed of members chosen every second year by the people of the several states, and the electors in each state shall have the qualifications requisite for electors of the most numerous branch of the state legislature.

(2) No person shall be a Representative who shall not have attained to the age of twenty five years, and been seven years a citizen of the United States, and who shall not, when elected, be an inhabitant of that state in which he shall be chosen.

(3) Representatives and direct taxes shall be apportioned among the several states which may be included within this union, according to their respective numbers, [which shall be determined by adding to the whole number of free persons, including those bound to service for a term of years, and excluding Indians not taxed, three fifths of all other persons]. The actual Enumeration shall be made within three years after the first meeting of the Congress of the United States, and within every subsequent term of ten years, in such manner as they shall by law direct. The number of Representatives shall not exceed one for every thirty thousand, but each state shall have at least one Representative; [and until such enumeration shall be made, the state of New Hampshire shall be entitled to chuse three, Massachusetts eight, Rhode Island and Providence Plantations one, Connecticut five, New York six, New Jersey four, Pennsylvania eight, Delaware one, Maryland six, Virginia ten, North Carolina five, South Carolina five, and Georgia three].

(4) When vacancies happen in the Representation from any state, the executive authority thereof shall issue writs of election to fill such vacancies.

(5) The House of Representatives shall choose their speaker and other officers; and shall have the sole power of impeachment.

The Senate

Section 3. (1) The Senate of the United States shall be composed of two Senators from each state, [chosen by the legislature thereof,] for six years; and each Senator shall have one vote.

(2) Immediately after they shall be assembled in consequence of the first election, they shall be divided as equally as may be into three classes. The seats of the Senators of the first class shall be vacated at the expiration of the second year, of the second class at the expiration of the fourth year, and the third class at the expiration of the sixth year, so that one third may be chosen every second year; [and if vacancies happen by resignation, or otherwise, during the recess of the legislature of any state, the executive thereof may make temporary appointments until the next meeting of the legislature, which shall then fill such vacancies].

(3) No person shall be a Senator who shall not have attained to the age of thirty years, and been nine years a citizen of the United States and who shall not, when elected, be an inhabitant of that state for which he shall be chosen.

(4) The Vice President of the United States shall be President of the Senate, but shall have no vote, unless they be equally divided.

(5) The Senate shall choose their other officers, and also a President *pro tempore,* in the absence of the Vice President, or when he shall exercise the office of President of the United States.

(6) The Senate shall have the sole power to try all impeachments. When sitting for that purpose, they shall be on oath or affirmation. When the President of the United States is tried, the Chief Justice shall preside: And no person shall be convicted without the concurrence of two thirds of the members present.

(7) Judgment in cases of impeachment shall not extend further than to removal from office, and disqualification to hold and enjoy any office of honor, trust or profit under the United States: but the party convicted shall nevertheless be liable and subject to indictment, trial, judgment and punishment, according to law.

Organization of Congress

Section 4. (1) The times, places and manner of holding elections for Senators and Representatives, shall be prescribed in each state by the legislature thereof; but the Congress may at any time by law make or alter such regulations, [except as to the places of choosing Senators].

(2) The Congress shall assemble at least once in every year, [and such meeting shall be on the first Monday in December], unless they shall by law appoint a different day.

Section 5. (1) Each House shall be the judge of the elections, returns and qualifications of its own members, and a majority of each shall constitute a quorum to do business; but a smaller number may adjourn from day to day, and may be authorized to compel the attendance of absent members, in such manner, and under such penalties as each House may provide.

(2) Each House may determine the rules of its proceedings, punish its members for disorderly behavior, and, with the concurrence of two thirds, expel a member.

(3) Each House shall keep a journal of its proceedings, and from time to time publish the same, excepting such parts as may in their judgment require secrecy; and the yeas and nays of the members of either House on any question shall, at the desire of one fifth of those present, be entered on the journal.

(4) Neither House, during the session of Congress, shall, without the consent of the other, adjourn for more than three days, nor to any other place than that in which the two Houses shall be sitting.

Section 6. (1) The Senators and Representatives shall receive a compensation for their services, to be ascertained by law, and paid out of the treasury of the United States. They shall in all cases, except treason, felony and breach of the peace, be privileged from arrest during their attendance at the session of their respective Houses, and in going to and returning from the same; and for any speech or debate in either House, they shall not be questioned in any other place.

(2) No Senator or Representative shall, during the time for which he was elected, be appointed to any civil office under the authority of the United States, which shall have been created, or the emoluments whereof shall have been increased during such time: and no person holding any office under the United States, shall be a member of either House during his continuance in office.

Section 7. (1) All bills for raising revenue shall originate in the House of Representatives; but the Senate may propose or concur with amendments as on other Bills.

(2) Every bill which shall have passed the House of Representatives and the Senate, shall, before it become a law, be presented to the President of the United States; if he approve he shall sign it, but if not he shall return it, with his objections to that House in which it shall have originated, who shall enter the objections at large on their journal, and proceed to reconsider it. If after such reconsideration two thirds of that House shall agree to pass the bill, it shall be sent, together with the objections, to the other House, by which it shall likewise be reconsidered, and if approved by two thirds of that House, it shall become a law. But in all such cases the votes of both Houses shall be determined by yeas and nays, and the names of the persons voting for and against the bill shall be entered on the journal of each House respectively. If any bill shall not be returned by the President within ten days (Sundays excepted) after it shall have been presented to him, the same shall be a law, in like manner as if he had signed it, unless the Congress by their

adjournment prevent its return, in which case it shall not be a law.

(3) Every order, resolution, or vote to which the concurrence of the Senate and House of Representatives may be necessary (except on a question of adjournment) shall be presented to the President of the United States; and before the same shall take effect, shall be approved by him, or being disapproved by him, shall be repassed by two thirds of the Senate and House of Representatives, according to the rules and limitations prescribed in the case of a bill.

POWERS GRANTED TO CONGRESS
The Congress shall have the power:

Section 8. (1) To lay and collect taxes, duties, imposts and excises, to pay the debts and provide for the common defense and general welfare of the United States; but all duties, imposts and excises shall be uniform throughout the United States;

(2) To borrow money on the credit of the United States;

(3) To regulate commerce with foreign nations, and among the several states, and with the Indian tribes;

(4) To establish a uniform rule of naturalization, and uniform laws on the subject of bankruptcies throughout the United States;

(5) To coin money, regulate the value thereof, and of foreign coin, and fix the standard of weights and measures;

(6) To provide for the punishment of counterfeiting the securities and current coin of the United States;

(7) To establish post offices and post roads;

(8) To promote the progress of science and useful arts, by securing for limited times to authors and inventors the exclusive right to their respective writings and discoveries;

(9) To constitute tribunals inferior to the Supreme Court;

(10) To define and punish piracies and felonies committed on the high seas, and offenses against the law of nations;

(11) To declare war, grant letters of marque and reprisal, and make rules concerning captures on land and water;

(12) To raise and support armies, but no appropriation of money to that use shall be for a longer term than two years;

(13) To provide and maintain a navy;

(14) To make rules for the government and regulation of the land and naval forces;

(15) To provide for calling forth the militia to execute the laws of the union, suppress insurrections and repel invasions;

(16) To provide for organizing, arming, and disciplining, the militia, and for governing such part of them as may be employed in the service of the United States, reserving to the states respectively, the appointment of the officers, and the authority of training the militia according to the discipline prescribed by Congress;

(17) To exercise exclusive legislation in all cases whatsoever, over such District (not exceeding ten miles square) as may, by cession of particular states, and the acceptance of Congress, become the seat of the government of the United States, and to exercise like authority over all places purchased by the consent of the legislature of the state in which the same shall be, for the erection of forts, magazines, arsenals, dockyards, and other needful buildings;—And

(18) To make all laws which shall be necessary and proper for carrying into execution the foregoing powers, and all other powers vested by this Constitution in the government of the United States, or in any department or officer thereof.

Powers Forbidden to Congress

Section 9. (1) The migration or importation of such persons as any of the states now existing shall think proper to admit, shall not be prohibited by the Congress prior to the year one thousand eight hundred and eight, but a tax or duty may be imposed on such importation, not exceeding ten dollars for each person.

(2) The privilege of the writ of *habeas corpus* shall not be suspended, unless when in cases of rebellion or invasion the public safety may require it.

(3) No bill of attainder or *ex post facto* Law shall be passed.

(4) No capitation, [or other direct,] tax shall be laid, unless in proportion to the census or enumeration herein before directed to be taken.

(5) No tax or duty shall be laid on articles exported from any state.

(6) No preference shall be given by any regulation of commerce or revenue to the ports of one state over those of another: nor shall vessels bound to, or from, one state, be obliged to enter, clear or pay duties in another.

(7) No money shall be drawn from the treasury, but in consequence of appropriations made by law; and a regular statement and account of receipts and expenditures of all public money shall be published from time to time.

(8) No title of nobility shall be granted by the United States: and no person holding any office of profit or trust under them, shall, without the consent of the Congress, accept of any present, emolument, office, or title, of any kind whatever, from any king, prince, or foreign state.

Powers Forbidden to the States

Section 10. (1) No state shall enter into any treaty, alliance, or confederation; grant letters of marque and reprisal; coin money; emit bills of credit; make any thing but gold and silver coin a tender in payment of debts; pass any bill of attainder, *ex post facto* law, or law impairing the obligation of contracts, or grant any title of nobility.

(2) No state shall, without the consent of the Congress, lay any imposts or duties on imports or exports, except what may be absolutely necessary for executing its inspection laws: and the net produce of all duties and imposts, laid by any state on imports or exports, shall be for the use of the treasury of the United States; and all such laws shall be subject to the revision and control of the Congress.

(3) No state shall, without the consent of Congress, lay any duty of tonnage, keep troops, or ships of war in time of peace, enter into any agreement or compact with another state, or with a foreign power, or engage in war, unless actually invaded, or in such imminent danger as will not admit of delay.

ARTICLE II
The Executive Branch

Section 1. (1) The executive power shall be vested in a President of the United States of America. He shall hold his office during the term of four years, and, together with the Vice President, chosen for the same term, be elected, as follows:

(2) Each state shall appoint, in such manner as the Legislature thereof may direct, a number of electors, equal to the whole number of Senators and Representatives to which the State may be entitled in the Congress: but no Senator or Representative, or person holding an office of trust or profit under the United States, shall be appointed an elector.

(3) [The electors shall meet in their respective states, and vote by ballot for two persons, of whom one at least shall not be an inhabitant of the same state with themselves. And they shall make a list of all the persons voted for, and of the number of votes for each; which list they shall sign and certify, and transmit sealed to the seat of the government of the United States, directed to the President of the Senate. The President of the Senate shall, in the presence of the Senate and House of Representatives, open all the certificates, and the votes shall then be counted. The person having the greatest number of votes shall be the President, if such number be a majority of the whole number of electors appointed; and if there be more than one who have such majority, and have an equal number of votes, then the House of Representatives shall immediately choose by ballot one of them for President; and if no person have a majority, then from the five highest on the list the said House shall in like manner choose the President. But in choosing the President, the votes shall be taken by States, the representation from each state having one vote; A quorum for this purpose shall consist of a member or members from two thirds of the states, and a majority of all the states shall be necessary to a choice. In every case, after the choice of the President, the person having the greatest number of votes of the electors shall be the Vice President. But if there should remain two or more who have equal votes, the Senate shall choose from them by ballot the Vice President.]

(4) The Congress may determine the time of choosing the electors, and the day on which they shall give their votes; which day shall be the same throughout the United States.

(5) No person except a natural born citizen, or a citizen of the United States, at the time of the adoption of this Constitution, shall be eligible to the office of President; neither shall any person be eligible to that office who shall not have attained to the age of thirty-five years, and been fourteen Years a resident within the United States.

(6) In case of the removal of the President from office, or of his death, resignation, or inability to discharge the powers and duties of the said office, the same shall devolve on the Vice President, and the Congress may by law provide for the case of removal, death, resignation or inability, both of the President and Vice President, declaring what officer shall then act as President, and such officer shall act accordingly, until the disability be removed, or a President shall be elected.

(7) The President shall, at stated times, receive for his services, a compensation, which shall neither be increased nor diminished during the period for which he shall have been elected, and he shall not receive within that period any other emolument from the United States, or any of them.

(8) Before he enter on the execution of his office, he shall take the following oath or affirmation:—"I do solemnly swear (or affirm) that I will faithfully execute the office of President of the United States, and will to the best of my ability, preserve, protect and defend the Constitution of the United States."

Section 2. (1) The President shall be commander in chief of the Army and Navy of the United States, and of the militia of the several states, when called into the actual service of the United States; he may require the opinion, in writing, of the principal officer in each of the executive departments, upon any subject relating to the duties of their respective offices, and he shall have power to grant reprieves and pardons for offenses against the United States, except in cases of impeachment.

(2) He shall have power, by and with the advice and consent of the Senate, to make treaties, provided two thirds of the Senators present concur; and he shall nominate, and by and with the advice and consent of the Senate, shall appoint ambassadors, other public ministers and consuls, judges of the Supreme Court, and all other officers of the United States, whose appointments are not herein otherwise provided for, and which shall be established by law: but the Congress may by law vest the appointment of such inferior officers, as they think proper, in the President alone, in the courts of law, or in the heads of departments.

(3) The President shall have power to fill up all vacancies that may happen during the recess of the Senate, by granting commissions which shall expire at the end of their next session.

Section 3. He shall from time to time give to the Congress information of the state of the union, and recommend to their consideration such measures as he shall judge necessary and expedient; he may, on extraordinary occasions, convene both Houses, or either of them, and in case of disagreement between them, with respect to the time of adjournment, he may adjourn them to such time as he shall think proper; he shall receive ambassadors and other public ministers; he shall take care that the laws be faithfully executed, and shall commission all the officers of the United States.

Section 4. The President, Vice President and all civil officers of the United States, shall be removed from office on impeachment for, and conviction of, treason, bribery, or other high crimes and misdemeanors.

ARTICLE III
The Judicial Branch

Section 1. The judicial power of the United States, shall be vested in one Supreme Court, and in such inferior courts as the Congress may from time to time ordain and establish. The judges, both of the supreme and inferior courts, shall hold their offices during good behaviour, and shall, at stated times, receive for their services, a compensation, which shall not be diminished during their continuance in office.

Section 2. (1) The judicial power shall extend to all cases, in law and equity, arising under this Constitution, the laws of the United States, and treaties made, or which shall be made, under their authority;—to all cases affecting ambassadors, other public ministers and consuls;—to all cases of admiralty and maritime jurisdiction;—to controversies to which the United States shall be a party;—to controversies between two or more states; [between a state and citizens of another state;]— between citizens of the same state, claiming lands under grants of different states, and between a state, or the citizens thereof, and foreign states, [citizens or subjects].

(2) In all cases affecting ambassadors, other public ministers and consuls, and those in which a state shall be party, the Supreme Court shall have original jurisdiction. In all the other cases before mentioned, the Supreme Court shall have appellate jurisdiction, both as to law and fact, with such exceptions, and under such regulations as the Congress shall make.

(3) The trial of all crimes, except in cases of impeachment, shall be by jury; and such trial shall be held in the state where the said crimes shall have been committed; but when not committed within any state, the trial shall be at such place or places as the Congress may by law have directed.

Section 3. (1) Treason against the United States, shall consist only in levying war against them, or in adhering to their enemies, giving them aid and comfort. No person shall be convicted of treason unless on the testimony of two witnesses to the same overt act, or on confession in open court.

(2) The Congress shall have power to declare the punishment of treason, but no attainder of treason shall work corruption of blood, or forfeiture except during the life of the person attainted.

ARTICLE IV
Relation of the States to Each Other

Section 1. Full faith and credit shall be given in each state to the public acts, records, and judicial proceedings of every other state. And the Congress may by general laws prescribe the manner in which such acts, records, and proceedings shall be proved, and the effect thereof.

Section 2. (1) The citizens of each state shall be entitled to all privileges and immunities of citizens in the several states.

(2) A person charged in any state with treason, felony, or other crime, who shall flee from justice, and be found in another state, shall on demand of the executive authority of the state from which he fled, be delivered up, to be removed to the state having jurisdiction of the crime.

(3) [No person held to service or labor in one state, under the laws thereof, escaping into another, shall, in consequence of any law or regulation therein, be discharged from such service or labor, but shall be delivered up on claim of the party to whom such service or labor may be due.]

Federal-State Relations

Section 3. (1) New states may be admitted by the Congress into this union; but no new states shall be formed or erected within the jurisdiction of any other state; nor any state be formed by the junction of two or more states, or parts of states, without the consent of the legislatures of the states concerned as well as of the Congress.

(2) The Congress shall have power to dispose of and make all needful rules and regulations respecting the territory or other property belonging to the United States; and nothing in this Constitution shall be so construed as to prejudice any claims of the United States, or of any particular state.

Section 4. The United States shall guarantee to every state in this union a republican form of government, and shall protect each of them against invasion; and on application of the legislature, or of the executive (when the legislature cannot be convened) against domestic violence.

ARTICLE V
Amending the Constitution

The Congress, whenever two thirds of both houses shall deem it necessary, shall propose amendments to this Constitution, or, on the application of the legislatures of two thirds of the several states, shall call a convention for proposing amendments, which, in either case, shall be valid to all intents and purposes, as part of this Constitution, when ratified by the legislatures of three fourths of the several states, or by conventions in three fourths thereof, as the one or the other mode of ratification may be proposed by the Congress; provided [that no amendment which may be made prior to the year one thousand eight hundred and eight shall in any manner affect the first and fourth clauses in the ninth section of the first article; and] that no state, without its consent, shall be deprived of its equal suffrage in the Senate.

ARTICLE VI
National Debts

(1) All debts contracted and engagements entered into, before the adoption of this Constitution, shall be as

valid against the United States under this Constitution, as under the Confederation.

Supremacy of the National Government

(2) This Constitution, and the laws of the United States which shall be made in pursuance thereof; and all treaties made, or which shall be made, under the authority of the United States, shall be the supreme law of the land; and the judges in every state shall be bound thereby, anything in the Constitution or laws of any State to the contrary notwithstanding.

(3) The Senators and Representatives before mentioned, and the members of the several state legislatures, and all executive and judicial officers, both of the United States and of the several states, shall be bound by oath or affirmation, to support this Constitution; but no religious test shall ever be required as a qualification to any office or public trust under the United States.

ARTICLE VII

Ratifying the Constitution

The ratification of the conventions of nine states, shall be sufficient for the establishment of this Constitution between the states so ratifying the same.

Done in convention by the unanimous consent of the states present the seventeenth day of September in the year of our Lord one thousand seven hundred and eighty seven and of the independence of the United States of America the twelfth. In witness whereof We have hereunto subscribed our Names.

Amendments to the Constitution

The first ten amendments, known as the Bill of Rights, were proposed on September 25, 1789. They were ratified, or accepted, on December 15, 1791. They were adopted because some states refused to approve the Constitution unless a Bill of Rights, protecting individuals from various unjust acts of government was added.

Amendment 1

Freedom of religion, speech, and the press; rights of assembly and petition

Amendment 2

Right to bear arms

Amendment 3

Housing of soldiers

Amendment 4

Search and arrest warrants

Amendment 5

Rights in criminal cases

Amendment 6

Rights to a fair trial

Amendment 7

Rights in civil cases

Amendment 8

Bails, fines, and punishments

Amendment 9

Rights retained by the people

Amendment 10

Powers retained by the states and the people

Amendment 11

Lawsuits against states

Amendment 12

Election of the President and Vice President

Amendment 13

Abolition of slavery

Amendment 14

Civil rights

Amendment 15

African-American suffrage

Amendment 16

Income taxes

Amendment 17

Direct election of senators

Amendment 18

Prohibition of liquor

Amendment 19

Women's suffrage

Amendment 20

Terms of the President and Congress

Amendment 21

Repeal of prohibition

Amendment 22

Presidential term limits

Amendment 23

Suffrage in the District of Columbia

Amendment 24

Poll taxes

Amendment 25

Presidential disability and succesion

Amendment 26

Suffrage for eighteen-year-olds

Amendment 27

Congressional salaries

Chapter Notes

Chapter 1. The Articles of Confederation

1. Milton Viorstre, ed., *The Great Documents of Western Civilization* (New York: Barnes & Noble Books: 1965), p.165.

Chapter 2. The Meeting That Changed the Nation

1. Christopher Collier and James Lincoln Collier, *Decision in Philadelphia: The Constitutional Convention of 1787* (New York: Ballantine Books, 1986), p. 55.

Chapter 3. The Framing of the Constitution

1. James Madison, *Writings* (New York: The Library of America, 1999), p. 90.

2. Jack N. Rakove, *Original Meanings: Politics and Ideas in the Making of the Constitution* (New York: Alfred A. Knopf, 1996), p. 106.

3. Thomas Fleming, *The Man Who Dared the Lightning: A New Look at Benjamin Franklin* (New York: William Morrow and Company, 1971), p. 486.

Chapter 4. Ratification

1. Eric Foner and John Garraty, eds., *The Reader's Companion to American History* (Boston: Houghton Mifflin Company, 1991) , p. 913.

2. Carl Van Doren, *The Great Rehearsal* (New York: The Viking Press, 1948), p. 180.

3. Christopher Collier and Hames Lincoln Collier, *Decision in Philadelphia: The Constitutional Convention of 1787* (New York: Ballantine Books, 1986) , p. 258.

Chapter 5. Concepts of the Constitution

1. Jerome B. Agel, ed., *Words That Make America Great* (New York: Random House, 1997), p. 217.

Chapter 6. The Bill of Rights

1. Andrew Carroll, ed., *Letters of a Nation* (New York: Kodansha International, 1997), pp. 76–77.

2. Leonard W. Levy, *Origins of the Bill of Rights* (New Haven, Conn.: Yale University Press, 1999), p. 35.

3. *New Jersey* v. *T.L.O.*, 469 U.S. 325 (1985).

Chapter 7. Adjustment and Extension of Rights

1. Henry Steele Commager, ed., *Document of American History*, 6th ed. (New York: Appleton-Century-Crofts, Inc., 1958), vol. 1, p. 161.

2. Geoffrey R. Stone, Louis M. Seidman, Cass R. Sunstein, and Mark V. Tushnet, *Constitutional Law*, 2nd ed. (Boston: Little, Brown and Company, 1991), p. 484.

3. Ibid., p. 486.

4. *The Constitution of the United States*, 18th ed. (Washington, D.C.: Commission on the Bicentennial of the United States Constitution, 1992), p. 34.

5. Louise Bernikow, *The American Women's Almanac: An Inspiring and Irreverent Women's History* (New York: Berkeley Books, 1997), p. 42.

Further Reading

Bradbury, Pamela and James Seward. *Men of the Constitution*. New York: Julian Messner, 1987.

The Commission on the Bicentennial of the United States Constitution. *1791–1991: The Bill of Rights and Beyond*. Washington, D.C.: U.S. Congress, 1991.

Dudley, William, ed. *The Creation of the Constitution: Opposing Viewpoints*. San Diego, Calif.: Greenhaven Press, Inc., 1995.

Faber, Doris and Harold Faber. *We the People: The Story of the United States Constitution Since 1787*. New York: Charles Scribner's Sons, 1987.

Feinberg, Barbara Silberdick. *The Articles of Confederation: The First Constitution of the United States*. Frederick, Md.: Twenty First Century Books, 2002.

Hull, Mary E. *Shays' Rebellion and the Constitution in American History*. Berkeley Heights, N.J.: Enslow Publishers, Inc., 2000.

Rosenburg, John. *First in Peace: George Washington, the Constitution, and the Presidency*. Brookfield, Conn.: Millbrook Press, 1998.

Internet Addresses

Congressional Research Service, Library of Congress. *The Constitution of the United States of America, Analysis and Interpretation.* <http://www.access.gpo.gov/congress/senate/constitution/toc.html>.

National Archives and Records Administration. *The Bill of Rights.* <http://www.archives.gov/exhibit_hall/charters_of_freedom/bill_of_rights/bill_of_rights.htm/>.

National Archives and Records Administration. *Constitution Day.* <http://www.archives.gov/digital_classroom/lessons/constitution_day/constitution_day.htm/>.

Index